W

JUL 3 1 2016

D0471120

Walla Walla
County Library

12 REASONS TO LOVE THE
NEW YORK YANKEES

by Doug Williams

J
796.357
William
2016

STORY
LIBRARY

www.12StoryLibrary.com

Copyright © 2016 by Peterson Publishing Company, North Mankato, MN 56003. All rights reserved. No part of this book may be reproduced or utilized in any form or by any means without written permission from the publisher.

12-Story Library is an imprint of Peterson Publishing Company and Press Room Editions.

Produced for 12-Story Library by Red Line Editorial

Photographs ©: Mark LoMoglio/Icon Sportswire/AP Images, cover, 1; Jason Aron/ Shutterstock Images, 4; Bettmann/Corbis, 5, 6, 9, 28; AP Images, 7, 13, 19, 27; Peter J. Carroll/AP Images, 10; Eugene Parciasepe/Shutterstock Images, 11; Saurabh13/ Shutterstock Images, 15, 29; Ray Stubblebine/AP Images, 16, 21; Charles Krupa/AP Images, 17; Adam Nadel/AP Images, 22; Scott Lomenzo/Shutterstock Images, 24; Ron Frehm/AP Images, 25; Daniel M. Silva/Shutterstock Images, 26

ISBN
978-1-63235-214-9 (hardcover)
978-1-63235-241-5 (paperback)
978-1-62143-266-1 (hosted ebook)

Library of Congress Control Number: 2015934319

Printed in the United States of America
Mankato, MN
October, 2015

Go beyond the book. Get free, up-to-date content on this topic at 12StoryLibrary.com.

TABLE OF CONTENTS

THE YANKEES ARE DRESSED TO THRILL IN NEW YORK

The New York Yankees are famous for their success. They have won more championships than any other Major League Baseball (MLB) team. They also are famous for their uniforms. For more than 100 years, their look has changed very little.

Theirs are one of the best-known uniforms in US sports.

The Yankees often are called "The Pinstripes." In 1912, thin, vertical stripes were added to the team's white home uniforms. These are called pinstripes.

Just a few years earlier, the team had adopted an interlocking N and Y as its logo. By 1912, that logo was displayed on the left chest of the uniforms. It was added to the caps, too. The uniform changed slightly in the 1920s and 1930s. But today, Yankees players wear a uniform similar to the one from 1912.

"You say pinstripes and the first thing that comes to most people's mind is the Yankees," said former New York shortstop Derek Jeter. "There's just

Derek Jeter in 2008

Babe Ruth (right) and Lou Gehrig pose in their Yankees pinstripes in 1927.

so much history there, and tradition."

In 1929, the Yankees became the first MLB team to make numbers a permanent part of their uniforms. Originally, the numbers indicated where the player hit in the batting order. The leadoff hitter was given No. 1. That's why slugger Babe Ruth, who batted third, wore No. 3.

All MLB teams have jersey numbers today. But Yankees uniforms remain unique in another way. The Yankees have the only uniforms that do not include the players' names on the backs of their home or road jerseys.

THINK ABOUT IT

Do you believe the Yankees have the best uniforms in baseball? Is there a better uniform? Write three or four sentences describing what makes a good uniform.

19

Seasons, from 1917 to 1935, in which the Yankees had no logo on their uniform. That span included Babe Ruth's entire Yankees career.

- The Yankees had several different cap designs from 1903 to 1922.
- They have worn their current dark blue caps since 1922.

5

"THE BAMBINO" CHANGES THE YANKEES

Until the Yankees acquired George Herman "Babe" Ruth after the 1919 season, they were just an average team. The team had been born in 1903 yet had never finished in first place. That finally changed when New York purchased Ruth from the Boston Red Sox.

Ruth had been a great pitcher and hitter in Boston. In New York, he became a full-time outfielder. In his first season with the Yankees in 1920, he hit 54 home runs. That broke his own record of 29 set the year before.

During the next three seasons, Ruth hit 59, 35, and 41 home runs respectively. Meanwhile, the Yankees won their first three American League (AL) championships. During his 15 seasons as a Yankee, the team won four World Series and seven AL pennants.

Ruth became baseball's biggest star. In 1927, he hit a record 60 home runs. That record wasn't broken until 1961. Ruth was so beloved by fans that even his nicknames had

Babe Ruth in 1926

nicknames. "The Babe" became known as "The Bambino." Fans also called him "The Sultan of Swat."

Ruth retired during the 1935 season. By then he was baseball's all-time leader in home runs with 714. But he was more than just a slugger. He won 94 games as a pitcher. And he was a colorful personality. He became a legend of the game. Today, a long home run is often described as "Ruthian." Ruth was part of the Baseball Hall of Fame's first induction class in 1936.

49

Average number of home runs hit by the seven other AL teams in 1921. Babe Ruth hit 59.

- Ruth led the AL in home runs 12 times.
- Ruth also led the league in walks 11 times.

"Babe Ruth was more than just the home run king," said hall of fame president Dale Petroskey. "He really was larger than life."

Babe Ruth hits one of his 714 home runs.

THE YANKEES RIDE THEIR "IRON HORSE"

Lou Gehrig became the Yankees' first baseman in 1925. He got his break when starter Wally Pipp took a day off because he was sick. Pipp never got his job back. Gehrig was so good and steady that he stayed in the Yankees' lineup for 2,130 consecutive games. His streak ended on May 2, 1939. That remained a record for consecutive games played until 1995.

During those 15 seasons, Gehrig was perhaps baseball's second-best slugger, behind only teammate Babe Ruth. Gehrig hit 493 home runs. He had at least 100 runs scored and 100 runs batted in (RBIs) for 13 consecutive seasons. His career batting average was .340.

Gehrig hit fourth in the lineup, right behind Ruth. Together they gave the Yankees a powerful one-two punch. Though both were left-handed power hitters, they were very different. Ruth was outspoken. Gehrig was quiet. He was the steady "Iron Horse."

THE BEST LINEUP EVER?

Lou Gehrig was the cleanup hitter for the 1927 Yankees. The team went 110–44 and won the AL title by 19 games. The lineup was so good it was called "Murderers' Row" for the damage it did to pitchers. It featured four hall of fame field players: Gehrig, outfielders Earle Combs and Babe Ruth, and second baseman Tony Lazzeri. Pitchers Waite Hoyt and Herb Pennock later went to the hall of fame, too. And so did manager Miller Huggins.

"He just went out and did his job every day," said Yankees catcher Bill Dickey.

To his teammates and fans, Gehrig seemed indestructible. Yet in 1938, he started to weaken. By the next year, he had to retire. A disease had attacked his muscles. Today that illness is commonly known as "Lou Gehrig's Disease."

Lou Gehrig follows through on a swing in 1927.

On July 4, 1939, Gehrig gave a retirement speech at Yankee Stadium.

"You have been reading about the bad break I got," Gehrig said. "Yet today I consider myself the luckiest man on the face of the earth. I have been in ballparks for 17 years and have never received anything but kindness and encouragement."

Gehrig was voted into the Baseball Hall of Fame that year. He died in 1941 at age 37.

23

Grand slams hit by Lou Gehrig, a record at the time.

- Gehrig had three of baseball's best six seasons for RBIs.
- Cal Ripken Jr. of the Baltimore Orioles broke Gehrig's consecutive games streak in 1995.

9

THE YANKEES WIN AND WIN AND WIN

Picking the best Yankees team is impossible. Would it be the 1927 "Murderers' Row" team? It won 110 games in the 154-game season. Then it swept the World Series in four games. Was it the 1961 team? It won 109 games. Or was it the 1998 team? It won a team-record 114 games and went 11–2 in the postseason.

The Yankees have won so many championships it's hard to choose. Their 27 World Series championships is a record. The St. Louis Cardinals rank second with 11. The Yankees also have won a record 40 AL pennants.

The Yankees were originally known as the Highlanders. They took on their current name in 1913. Soon after, they took off. They won their first league pennant in 1921. After that, they won league championships in every decade of the 20th century. The Yankees won World Series titles in every decade but the 1980s. They also won two in the 2000s.

The early champion teams were built around hitters Babe Ruth and

Yankees (from left) Roger Maris, Yogi Berra, and Mickey Mantle in 1961

Lou Gehrig with pitchers Herb Pennock and Waite Hoyt. In the 1930s and 1940s, Joe DiMaggio was the star. Then came the 1950s and 1960s. Outfielder Mickey Mantle, catcher Yogi Berra, and pitcher Whitey Ford helped the Yankees dominate. In the 1970s, outfielder Reggie Jackson, catcher Thurman Munson, and pitcher Ron Guidry were the biggest names. In the 1990s and into the 2000s, shortstop Derek Jeter and closer

Mariano Rivera helped New York win five World Series.

Players feel the winning tradition when they put on the Yankees' uniform. When third baseman Chase Headley joined the team in 2014, he sensed it. Said Headley, "There's a mystique, an aura, a tradition of success, that's different than any other organization."

10

World Series championships won by Yankees catcher Yogi Berra from 1947 to 1962. No player has won more.

- The Yankees played in the World Series in 16 of 18 years from 1947 to 1964.
- Berra was on all 10 winning teams during that stretch.
- The Yankees won a record five World Series in a row from 1949 to 1953.

Mariano Rivera pitches while Derek Jeter looks on in a 2003 game.

5

THE AMAZING GRACE OF JOE DiMAGGIO

Joe DiMaggio had style. He ran with speed and grace. His swing was beautiful. He hit the ball far. He rarely made a mistake in center field. Even his teammates were in awe.

"There was an aura about him," said Yankees shortstop Phil Rizzuto. "He walked like no one else walked. He did things so easily."

DiMaggio was just 21 when he arrived in New York in 1936. But the kid from San Francisco was not overwhelmed. In his first season, he hit .323. In 1937, his 46 home runs led the AL. By the time he was 26, he had won two batting championships and two AL Most Valuable Player (MVP) Awards. But his greatest feat came in 1941. DiMaggio had a record 56-game hitting streak that year. It's never been matched.

During his 13-year career, DiMaggio had a lifetime batting average of .325 with 361 home runs. Other

A POP CULTURE STAR

To his generation, Joe DiMaggio was more than a baseball player. He married one of Hollywood's biggest stars, Marilyn Monroe, in 1954. The media called it "the marriage of the century." Ernest Hemingway included DiMaggio in his 1952 novel, *The Old Man and the Sea*. In baseball's 100th anniversary in 1969, DiMaggio was voted baseball's greatest living player.

Joe DiMaggio records a hit in his 42nd consecutive game during the 1941 season.

players and fans raved about the way he played. He was "The Yankee Clipper"—a smooth, athletic star.

Boston Red Sox star Ted Williams said DiMaggio "was the greatest all-around player I ever saw." Yankees catcher Yogi Berra said DiMaggio was always in the right place at the right time. "He never did anything wrong on the field," said Berra.

369

Number of times Joe DiMaggio struck out, an average of just 28 times per season.

- DiMaggio added a third AL MVP Award in 1947.
- He missed the 1943 to 1945 seasons while serving in World War II.

YANKEE STADIUM IS A PARK WITH RICH HISTORY

Since 1923, the Yankees' ballpark has been called Yankee Stadium. That year, the Yankees played for the first time in their home park in the Bronx, a section of New York City. At the end of the 2008 season, the stadium closed. In 2009, the Yankees moved into their new home, next to the old one. This park often is referred to as "new" Yankee Stadium.

Though the stadium has been upgraded, it's much like the old one. The top of the upper deck is decorated with the same facade. It's a white, decorative steel pattern that hangs from the roof. It was added to the original park to give it "an air of dignity."

New Yankee Stadium also includes other features of the old stadium. One is the short porch in right field. The fence down the right-field line has been closer to home plate than the left-field wall for most of the stadium's history. The design allowed the Yankees to take advantage of the left-handed power of Lou Gehrig and Babe Ruth. In fact, Ruth hit a home run in the Yankees' first game at Yankee Stadium in 1923. The park often was called "The House That Ruth Built."

THINK ABOUT IT

If you could redesign Yankee Stadium, would you change the dimensions? Should it be so easy to hit home runs to right field but so hard to hit them to left and center? Write three or four sentences to explain your answer.

The new Yankee Stadium

Through the years, the distance to the short porch increased to 314 feet, but it is still closer than in most parks. It's one of the reasons most of the Yankees' greatest sluggers have been left-handed, including Ruth, Gehrig, Roger Maris, Mickey Mantle (a switch hitter), and Reggie Jackson.

$1.3 billion

Cost to build the new Yankee Stadium.

- The original Yankee Stadium cost $2.5 million.
- The Yankees previously played at the Polo Grounds and Hilltop Park.
- They played two seasons at Shea Stadium, the home of the New York Mets, in the 1970s.

A MONUMENT TO GREATNESS

Beyond the left-field fence in new Yankee Stadium is Monument Park. It's an area that honors the greatest Yankees. There are six large stone monuments in the park. Twenty-four plaques and 20 retired numbers are displayed on walls. It is one of the most popular places for fans to visit.

15

THE YANKEES AND RED SOX FACE OFF IN THE FIERCEST RIVALRY

The New York Yankees' first year was 1903. The Boston Red Sox began play in 1901. Back then, the New York team was called the Highlanders. The Boston team was called the Americans.

Much has changed since, including the teams' names. But one thing hasn't. The Yankees and Red Sox remain fierce rivals. There are many reasons. The cities are just 190 miles (306 km) apart. The fans of both teams are passionate. And many times, league and division championships have been decided by games between the two teams.

Former baseball commissioner Bud Selig called it "the greatest rivalry in sports." Some believe the rivalry really began in late 1919. That's when the Red Sox sold Babe Ruth to the Yankees. Before that, the Red Sox had won five

Bucky Dent homers against the Red Sox in the one-game playoff to decide the 1978 AL East title.

World Series.
Since then,
the Yankees
have won 27
World Series. Boston
didn't win its sixth until 2004.

Derek Jeter homers against the Red Sox during the 2003 ALCS.

The rivalry has had many memorable moments over the years. In 1949, the Red Sox needed to win just one of their final two games of the season against New York to win the pennant. But the Yankees won both. In 1978, the Red Sox had a 14-game lead over the Yankees in July. Yet when the regular season ended, they were tied. That forced a one-game playoff. The Yankees won it 5–4 on a home run by light-hitting shortstop Bucky Dent.

In 2002, Red Sox president Larry Lucchino angered the Yankees by calling them "The Evil Empire." One year later, the Yankees' Aaron Boone hit an 11th-inning home run in Game 7 of the AL Championship Series (ALCS) to defeat Boston. A year later, the Red Sox fell behind the Yankees three games to none in the ALCS. Then Boston won four straight.

17
Longest winning streak between the teams in their long rivalry.

- The Red Sox won 17 straight games against the Yankees in 1911 and 1912.
- The teams have met three times in the playoffs, with the Yankees winning twice.

17

MARIS WINS EXCITING HOME RUN CHASE

The 1961 Yankees team was one of the best in team history. The team went 109–53. The Yankees then won the World Series in five games over the Cincinnati Reds.

That Yankees team hit 240 home runs. It stood as a record until 1996. Six Yankees hit at least 20 homers. And future hall of fame player Whitey Ford went 25–4 to lead a strong pitching staff. Yet it all was overshadowed by two Yankees outfielders. Mickey Mantle and Roger Maris captured attention all year as they chased Babe Ruth's season home run record. The two picked up the nickname "The M&M Boys." Mantle hit third in the lineup. Maris hit fourth.

For months, it appeared both might break Ruth's record of 60 home runs. By mid-August, they each had 45. In September, Mantle suffered an injury. He finished with 54. Maris,

THE ASTERISK

The AL season was 162 games in 1961. Babe Ruth had set his home run record in a 154-game season. So some argued that Roger Maris hadn't broken Ruth's mark. Baseball Commissioner Ford Frick ruled that Maris's achievement required a "distinctive mark" in the record book. For many years, Maris's record was said to have an asterisk next to it. But in 1991, a major league committee ruled no distinction should be made.

meanwhile, hit 10 home runs in the final month. His 60th home run tied Ruth in the 159th game. He hit No. 61 in the final game of the regular season.

Maris had felt the pressure of the home run chase. But after his home run, he smiled at the crowd and tipped his cap as Yankees fans cheered.

Roger Maris hits his 60th home run of the 1961 season.

115

Combined home runs by Mickey Mantle and Roger Maris in 1961, a season record for teammates.

- The St. Louis Cardinals' Mark McGwire broke Maris's record in 1998.
- San Francisco Giants outfielder Barry Bonds now holds the record with 73 home runs hit in 2001.
- Both McGwire and Bonds were later linked to illegal performance-enhancing drugs.

THINK ABOUT IT

Pretend you are a Yankees fan in 1961. Babe Ruth was a beloved player. You might have thought his single-season home run record would last forever. How would you feel about Roger Maris breaking the record? Write a few sentences to explain your thoughts.

YANKEE STADIUM BECOMES "THE BRONX ZOO"

The period of the late 1970s and early 1980s was among the wildest in Yankees history.

It was a successful era. From 1976 through 1981, the Yankees won four AL pennants and two World Series. The lineup was filled with All-Stars, such as catcher Thurman Munson, outfielder Reggie Jackson, and third baseman Graig Nettles. Ron Guidry, Jim "Catfish" Hunter, and Tommy John were excellent starting pitchers. And Rich "Goose" Gossage was a great closer.

But it also was a crazy time. Players fought with their manager. Owner George Steinbrenner feuded with everyone. Almost every day, there was a new controversy. Media in New York said Yankee Stadium was home to "The Bronx Zoo."

Several famous incidents occurred during this era. Many involved Jackson. The slugger joined the team as a free agent in 1977. Soon after, he criticized Munson. Jackson called himself "the straw that stirs the drink." He said Munson "thinks he can be the straw that stirs the drink, but he can only stir it bad."

4

Consecutive at-bats in which Reggie Jackson hit a home run in the 1977 World Series.

- He hit five home runs in six games.
- Jackson was selected World Series MVP as the Yankees beat the Los Angeles Dodgers.

Yankees owner George Steinbrenner holds a press conference in 1982.

The comments turned many of his teammates against him.

Jackson and manager Billy Martin clashed often. They even fought in the dugout during a 1977 game. But Martin and Steinbrenner clashed more often. From 1975 to 1988, Steinbrenner hired Martin five times. He fired him five times.

Said Nettles, "When I was a little boy, I wanted to be a baseball player and join the circus. With the Yankees, I have accomplished both."

HE WAS THE BOSS

When George Steinbrenner bought the Yankees in 1973, he took command. His nickname was "The Boss." He spent big money on star free agents. He publicly criticized players and managers. And he feuded with Reggie Jackson and Billy Martin. "Each one of them wanted to be their own boss," said Yankees third baseman Graig Nettles.

THE BLEACHER CREATURES HOLD DOWN RIGHT FIELD

Yankees fans always have been loud. They cheer for good plays. They boo mistakes. Often they insult visiting players. They never have been shy about expressing their feelings. It creates an exciting and interesting atmosphere at Yankee Stadium.

Over the years, the fans in right field have been the loudest of all. Since

Fans celebrate from the right field bleachers at Yankee Stadium after the Yankees won Game 1 of the 1998 World Series.

the early 1980s, fans in a specific area of right field have been called "The Bleacher Creatures." They have been called the "rowdiest collection of baseball fans anywhere."

During games, Bleacher Creature fans take part in chants. At the start of games, they have the roll call. Together they call out to each Yankees player at his position until he waves to them.

Often they poke fun at the visiting team's right fielder. Sometimes they have thrown objects at players. Occasionally, fans in the area get into fights.

"You could throw raw meat out there and they'll eat it," said former Oakland A's right fielder Jose Canseco. "It's wild."

Ichiro Suzuki of Japan made his first appearance in right field for the Seattle Mariners at Yankee Stadium in 2001. Some Creatures learned insults in Japanese to yell at him.

After Robinson Cano left the Yankees to sign with Seattle, the Creatures booed and taunted him when he returned. They chanted, "You sold out!"

9

Years beer sales were banned in the Bleacher Creature section, starting in 2000.

- Officials blamed beer for the Bleacher Creatures' rowdy behavior.
- In old Yankee Stadium, the official Bleacher Creature area was in Sections 37 and 39.
- Since the new stadium opened in 2009, the Creatures sit in Section 203.

THINK ABOUT IT

Do you believe the Bleacher Creatures make it more fun to attend a game? Or does it spoil the game? Write three or four sentences to explain your answer.

DEREK JETER WAS GREAT RIGHT FROM THE START

In 1992, the Yankees were considering drafting high school shortstop Derek Jeter from Michigan. Yankees scout Dick Groch was convinced Jeter should be taken with the team's sixth overall choice.

When Groch was asked if Jeter might play at the University of Michigan instead of signing with the Yankees, he said no.

"The only place he's going is Cooperstown," said Groch.

Derek Jeter connects on a pitch during a game at Yankee Stadium.

Groch was correct. Cooperstown, New York, is the home of the Baseball Hall of Fame. In a 20-year major league career, Jeter proved he belonged

THINK ABOUT IT

The Yankees have had several different superstars in their most successful eras. Which one do you think was the best? Use this book to find evidence to support your answer.

200

Hits by Derek Jeter in 158 postseason games, a record. Yankee Bernie Williams is second with 128.

- Jeter, catcher Jorge Posada, and pitchers Andy Pettitte and Mariano Rivera were called the "Core Four."
- They all joined the Yankees organization in the early 1990s and helped the Yankees win four World Series.
- Jeter, Posada, and Rivera played together from 1995 to 2011.

among the greats. Jeter had 3,465 hits—the sixth best total in history. He's the Yankees' all-time leader in hits, games played, doubles, and stolen bases.

From his first full season in 1996, Jeter made an impact. He batted .314 and was selected AL Rookie of the Year. He hit at least .300 10 times. He was a 14-time All-Star. He won five Gold Gloves for his fielding. And he helped the Yankees win five World Series.

Derek Jeter makes a leaping throw to first base during a 1998 playoff game.

Jeter always seemed to get the big hit or make the big play. Because he had been named the team's 11th captain in 2003, fans called him "The Captain."

NEW YORK IS RUNNING OUT OF NUMBERS

It's hard for a new Yankees player to get a good jersey number. That's because the Yankees have retired 20 numbers representing 22 great players and managers.

No single-digit uniform numbers are available. The numbers of manager Billy Martin (1), outfielder Babe Ruth (3), first baseman Lou Gehrig (4), outfielder Joe DiMaggio (5), manager Joe Torre (6), outfielder Mickey Mantle (7), catchers Yogi Berra and Bill Dickey (8), and outfielder Roger Maris (9) are retired. Shortstop Derek Jeter's No. 2 is no longer issued. It will be retired, too.

Seventeen players who spent most of their careers as Yankees are in the Baseball Hall of Fame. Overall, 40 players and managers who wore Yankee pinstripes are in the hall.

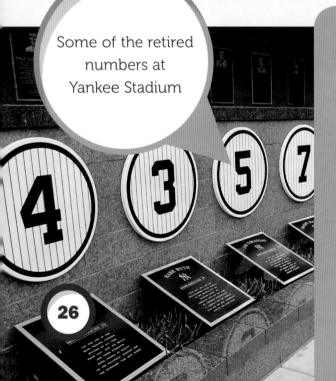

Some of the retired numbers at Yankee Stadium

1,785
Games played by first baseman Don Mattingly without playing in a World Series, a team record.

- The Yankees had nine hall of fame players on the team every year from 1930 to 1933.
- They had at least one hall of fame player on the team every year from 1913 to 1968.

PERFECT IN PINSTRIPES

Yankees pitchers Don Larsen and David Wells both achieved perfection. A perfect game occurs when no batters reach base by a hit or walk. Larsen was perfect in the fifth game of the 1956 World Series. His performance helped the Yankees beat the Brooklyn Dodgers 2–0. It's the only perfect game in World Series history. In 1998, Wells pitched a perfect game to beat the Minnesota Twins 4–0. Both Larsen and Wells attended the same high school in San Diego.

The list includes superstars such as Ruth and Mantle. But there were many other key players, too. Starting pitcher Whitey Ford is the team's all-time leader in wins. Ford went 236–106 over 16 seasons in the 1950s and 1960s. Center fielder Earle Combs batted .325 in the 1920s and 1930s. That is the third-highest batting average in team history. Meanwhile, Mariano Rivera set the standard for closers in the 1990s and 2000s. He saved 652 regular-season games and 42 postseason games. Both are records.

Yankees catcher Yogi Berra jumps into Don Larsen's arms after Larsen's perfect game in the 1956 World Series.

12 KEY DATES

1903

After the Baltimore team of the AL folds, a new AL team begins play in New York. Because the team plays at one of the highest spots on Manhattan, it takes on the nickname Highlanders.

1913

The team is renamed the Yankees. Local sportswriters introduced the name because it was easier to fit on headlines.

1923

Yankees slugger Babe Ruth hits a home run in a 4–1 win over the Boston Red Sox on April 18 in the first game at Yankee Stadium.

1923

The Yankees beat the New York Giants to clinch their first World Series championship on October 15.

1939

Lou Gehrig's consecutive games streak comes to an end at 2,130 on May 2.

1941

After hitting in 56 straight games, Joe DiMaggio goes 0-for-3 in a victory over the Cleveland Indians on July 17.

1946

The first night game is played at Yankee Stadium on May 28.

1956
Don Larsen pitches a perfect game against the Brooklyn Dodgers in Game 5 of the World Series on October 8. The Yankees win 2–0.

1961
Roger Maris hits his 61st home run on October 1 to break Ruth's record set in 1927.

1973
George Steinbrenner buys controlling interest of the Yankees on January 3.

2009
The new Yankee Stadium opens on April 16 with the Cleveland Indians beating the hosts 10–2.

2009
Yankees win their 27th World Series, defeating the Philadelphia Phillies in six games.

GLOSSARY

closer
A pitcher who typically pitches in the final inning, especially when his team is winning.

commissioner
The executive in charge of MLB.

facade
The face of a building.

free agent
A player who is free to sign with any team.

manager
The person in charge of the team during games.

media
People who work in the mass communication industry at places such as newspapers, magazines, and TV stations.

pennant
A league championship.

postseason
Games played after the regular season, including wild-card, divisional, and league championship games, plus the World Series.

retire
To end one's career. A team can also retire a number to honor an iconic player, meaning no future player on that team can wear the number again.

short porch
A slang term for an outfield fence that is close to home plate, making it a welcome target for home run hitters.

FOR MORE INFORMATION

Books

Frommer, Harvey. *A Yankee Century & Beyond.* New York: The Berkley
Publishing Group, 2007.

Pepe, Phil. *Core Four: The Heart and Soul of the Yankees Dynasty.*
Chicago: Triumph Books, 2013.

Torre, Joe, and Tom Verducci. *The Yankee Years.* New York: Anchor Books,
2010.

Websites

Baseball Hall of Fame
www.baseballhall.org

Baseball Reference
www.baseball-reference.com

New York Yankees
www.newyork.yankees.mlb.com

INDEX

About the Author

Doug Williams is a freelance writer in San Diego, California. He is a former newspaper reporter and editor. He's written several books about sports and writes for many national and San Diego-area publications. He is a lifelong baseball fan.

READ MORE FROM 12-STORY LIBRARY

Every 12-Story Library book is available in many formats, including Amazon Kindle and Apple iBooks. For more information, visit your device's store or 12StoryLibrary.com.